LET'S INVESTIGATE

TRACING YOUR FAMILY TREE

Published in this edition by Peter Haddock Ltd, Pinfiold Lane,
Bridlington, East Yorkshire YO16 5BT

ISBN 0 7105 0977 4

Printed and bound in India

PART ONE

STARTING YOUR TREE

Have you ever wondered how far back you could trace your family? Who your grandfather's father was, where he lived and what he did? Finding this out is called tracing your family tree. It is called a tree because it is like climbing a tree. You start at the bottom and climb, branch by branch, as high as you can go.

It can be made into a very exciting game of detectives, and, like a detective, you begin by putting down all the facts that you already know before looking for clues that will take you further back. But first you must get together your equipment.

Project

Prepare for action

Start collecting:

- pencils and notebooks
- large-size paper for the tree when complete
- a magnifying glass for deciphering old and fading records, and names on old tombstones
- a ruler and coloured pencils to show up the different lines in the tree

- an envelope file or box file, if more than one tree is being attempted, in which to keep the actual trees
- a camera.

Project

The first step

Put the word 'Clues' on the front of your notebook. On the first page put 'Bottom of my tree', because, as you know all about yourself, you will be at the bottom with your brothers and sisters. Start by sticking in a photograph of yourself, and underneath put down all the interesting things about yourself. Do exactly the same for your brothers and sisters if you have any (*see* figure 1). If you have any cousins, they will also go at the bottom of the tree, which will grow beside yours. You can start their tree in the same way when you have finished yours, and you will find that it will join up with your grandparents on the second branch.

Figure 1

Bottom of my tree

brother	me	sister	sister

Project

Climb to a branch

When you have done this, head a page ‘First branch’ (*see* figure 2). On this will be your mother and father. You do the same about them, but here you will have to start being a proper detective, because you will have to question them, and take down each of their statements. Such as—Where were you born? Have you any brothers and sisters? What are their names? What is your work? When and where did you get married? Where did you live before you got married? Remember to ask your mother her surname before she got married, where she lived and what work she did.

Figure 2

First branch

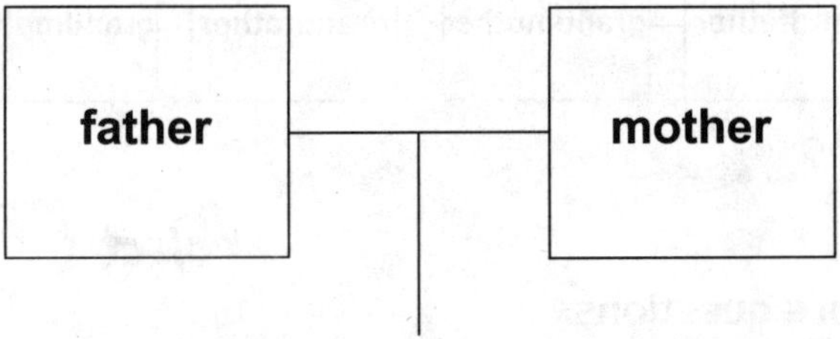

Project

Ask your uncles and aunts

Next ask for photographs of your uncles and aunts and

ask them questions too. They will go with your cousins, on their own tree, which will be linked to yours.

Project

Up to the second branch

When you have finished the first branch, put 'Second branch' on a separate page, and on this will go your grandfathers and grandmothers (*see* figure 3). *You* can make them a little more interesting by finding two pictures of them. One showing them as they are now, and one showing them as they looked when they were younger.

Second branch

Figure 3

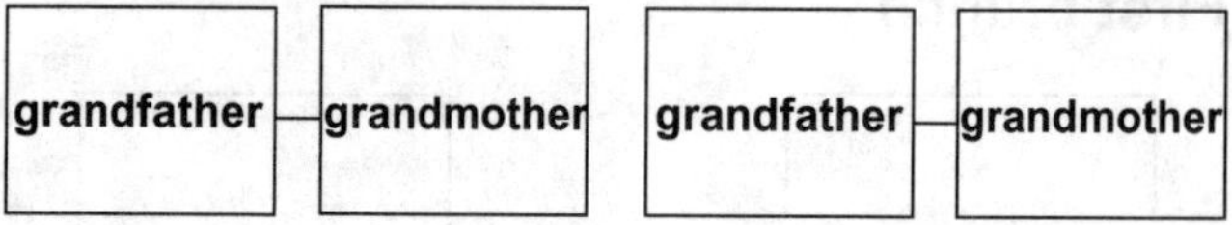

Project

More questions

Ask each of your grandparents a lot of questions. Here are a few extra ones that will help you build up your 'Third branch' when you get to it:

- Where were you born?

- Who were your parents?
- Where were they born and when?
- Where were they married and when?
- What were the names of your brothers and sisters?
- What were the names of your uncles and aunts?
- What work did these people do?

Ask them for photographs of their brothers and sisters, and their fathers and mothers, and ask them questions about them too. You are getting quite far back now, and you may find that they were old craftsmen whose crafts have died out now that machinery has taken over the work. If you find the village or small town in which your ancestors lived, you may be able to see some of the work they actually did, like a carving in a church or wrought-iron work.

Project

Get your camera

Take photographs, or draw pictures, of your family's old homes and of their gravestones, because these often have very interesting information on them.

Old people often love to talk about their younger days, their homes and their families, and what they did together. Ask them if they have any old photographs of the town and village they used to live in and see how it has changed over the years.

Project

For your notebook

Take notes on everything they tell you, even if it sounds unimportant, because anything may be a clue to something you want to find out later on in your search. Remember also that after so many years they may have forgotten a few things, so you will have to check their evidence. Ask their old friends some questions too—they may remember things your grandparents have forgotten.

A very important question is the one about where they got married, because most people get married in the home town of the bride, and this will be a clue as to where your grandmother, or whoever it is you are tracing, lived.

You may even be lucky enough to find one of your relations has an old family bible, in which it was often the custom to record all births, marriages and deaths.

Now you will have a book full of information and clues, and you can start building up your family tree properly.

Project

Start the climb

Now let us start the climb. You will know your own birthday, and the names and birthdays of your brothers and sisters, so put yourself and them on the bottom, putting the eldest first, and then the next in order of age. Put the dates and places of your births under each name, like David and Mary in figure 4.

Make sure you have enough room to fit all the information in by writing the dates in a shortened form. Use numbers to record firstly the day, then the month and finally the year. For example, if you were born on the fifteenth of April in 1984 then this would be shortened to 15/4/84.

Figure 4

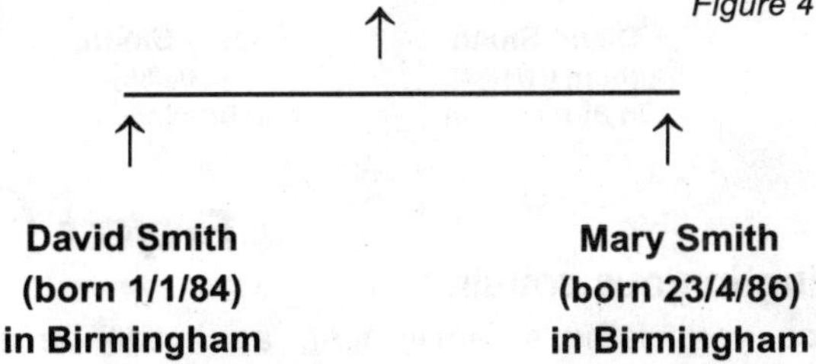

Project

The second stage

You will notice that the arrows point up to the first branch, on which will be the names of your father and mother. Let's call them David and Mary too, because you will find that the further back you go, and up the tree, families tended to name their children after their parents. The tree now looks like figure 5.

Figure 5

David Smith—m—Mary Jones (3/3/81) in Chester
(born 5/2/55 in Chester) **(born 16/6/57 in Chester)**

David Smith (born 01/1/84) in Birmingham

Mary Smith (23/4/86) in Birmingham

Project

Bring in your cousins

Trace your father's family first, as it will be easier because his surname will be the same all the way up, whereas women usually change their surnames when they get married. If your father has a brother, we will call him William. His name, and that of his wife will go on the same branch as your father's, like your brothers and sisters on the bottom line. Uncle William's children will be your cousins and will go at the bottom of the tree, as in figure 6.

Ignore your cousins because they will have their own tree growing beside yours.

Figure 6

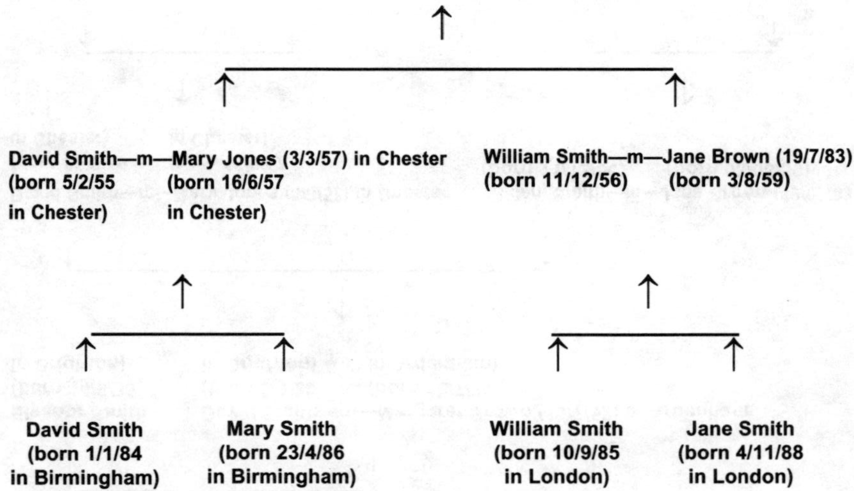
David Smith—m—Mary Jones (3/3/57) in Chester
(born 5/2/55 in Chester)
(born 16/6/57 in Chester)
William Smith—m—Jane Brown (19/7/83)
(born 11/12/56)
(born 3/8/59)
David Smith (born 1/1/84 in Birmingham)
Mary Smith (born 23/4/86 in Birmingham)
William Smith (born 10/9/85 in London)
Jane Smith (born 4/11/88 in London)

Figure 7

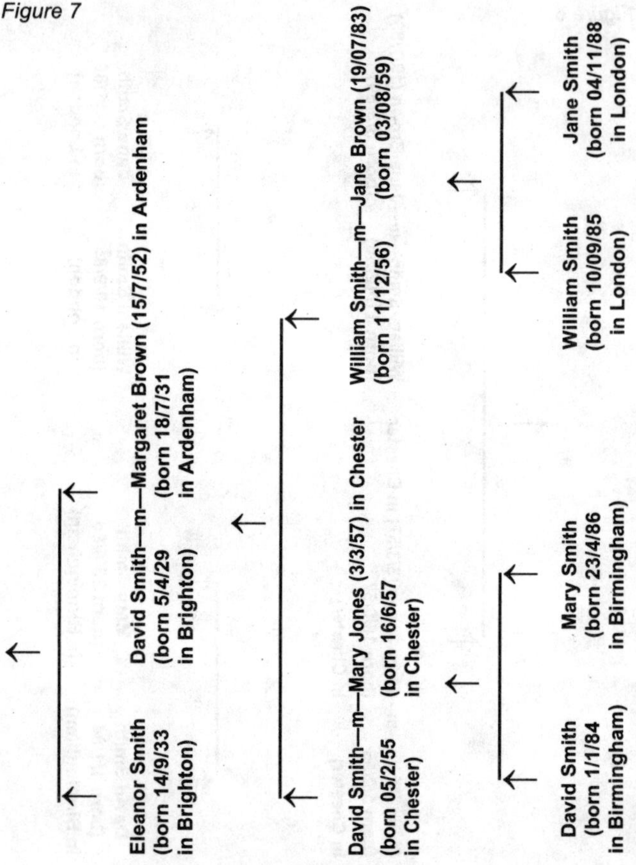

Eleanor Smith
(born 14/9/33
in Brighton)
David Smith—m—Margaret Brown (15/7/52) in Ardenham
(born 5/4/29
in Brighton)
(born 18/7/31
in Ardenham)
David Smith—m—Mary Jones (3/3/57) in Chester
(born 05/2/55
in Chester)
(born 16/6/57
in Chester)
William Smith—m—Jane Brown (19/07/83)
(born 11/12/56)
(born 03/08/59)
David Smith
(born 1/1/84
in Birmingham)
Mary Smith
(born 23/4/86
in Birmingham)
William Smith
(born 10/09/85
in London)
Jane Smith
(born 04/11/88
in London)

Project

Add more branches

The second branch of your tree will have on it the names of your grandparents (your father's father and mother, if it is his family you are starting with) and the names of your grandfather's brothers and sisters. In this way you go on adding to your tree, branch by branch, and watch it grow, as in figure 7.

Project

Three branches of a tree

In figure 8 there is a photograph of three branches on a family tree. See if you can make one like it, and make a

Figure 8

note of all the names on it. If you have great-grandparents include them too, then you will have a photograph of four branches of a family tree. This could go in your personal notebook to mark the end of your questioning.

PART TWO

WHERE TO CHECK YOUR EVIDENCE

Having asked all the questions you can think of, and this may even mean writing letters to those in your family who live far away, you should have a notebook full of clues. The next step is to check your evidence and find more clues to help your tree to spread. There are several ways of doing this, and the first step is to look for records, or make a 'search', in St Catherine's House, in London.

Project

Visit the search rooms

If you live near London or are on a visit it is best to go to St Catherine's House yourself. The Search Rooms of the General Register Office are open from 8.30 am to 4.30 pm, Monday to Friday.

Until 1837, all records of baptisms, marriages and deaths were left to the local clergy, some of whom kept their records very well, but others either forgot them or wrote them down on odd scraps of paper that were then lost. The further back you go the more muddled some of them become.

Also, you will notice that it was baptisms, the day on which the child was baptised (or christened), they recorded, not births, so it can sometimes be difficult to find the year of a birth.

In 1837, however, it was made law for all records of births, marriages and deaths to be kept in England and Wales by local registrars, who keep the originals, and give a copy each to the local minister and the Registrar General in London. The local registers are open to the public but cover only local records, whereas at St Catherine's House, where they will supply you with a copy for a fee of £6, they cover the whole of England and Wales.

These central records are kept in the Office of Population Censuses and Surveys, General Register Office. If you wish to make a search at St Catherine's House, you can do so free. However, you will not be able to look at the original registers. You are allowed to search the indexes of names to find the entry you are searching for. Having found the relevant entry you can then apply for a copy of the certificate.

Project

First find the index

If you are going to make a search at St Catherine's House it is necessary to take as much information as possible, written down in your notebook. This will save you time and money in finding and applying for the relevant certificates. For example, if you are searching for the birth certificate of somebody with the name David Brown, it might be that another David Brown was registered in the same district and in the same quarter of the year. Therefore, it is best to have as much information as possible about your David Brown before you begin your search.

Before 1984 the indexes are arranged in quarters—so if you were born in February 1982, you would need to search the index for March 1982, which covers the months January, February and March of that year. The June index covers April, May and June, and so on. From 1984 onwards the indexes are compiled for a full year. In all the indexes the entries are compiled alphabetically by surname and forename. The indexes will also give the name of the Superintendent Registrar's District that corresponds to the area in which the birth was registered. You can double-check that you have the right district by consulting material available in the General Register Office, which gives the locations of the registration districts.

When searching quarterly indexes it is important to remember that a birth is not always registered on the day that a child is born. By law a birth can be registered up to 42 days after the actual date of birth. So it might be that the certificate of somebody born in March will be found in the index for the June quarter. Once you have found the entry that you are sure is the one for you, the next step is to apply for a copy of the certificate

Project

Fill in your form

To apply for a copy of the certificate you will need to fill in a form with the name at birth, and the date and place of birth of the child, and particulars of the parents. A full certificate will provide the following information:

- name, sex, date of birth and address of the child
- the name and occupation of the child's father at the time of registration
- the name and maiden name of the child's mother, that is her name before she was married
- the date on which the birth was registered
- the name and the address of the individual supplying the information to the registrar

A short certificate contains only the name, sex, date of birth and place of birth of the child.

You will also need to supply your details as an applicant—name, full postal address and telephone number—so that the copy of the certificate can then be sent out to you if you are not going to collect it in person. This will take a few days. There is a service available that provides a certificate within 24 hours. This is much more expensive, so it is worth waiting a few days.

Figure 9: An example of a full birth certificate

NHS Number | **BIRTH** | Entry No. 137

Registration district NEWTOWN | Administrative Area

Sub-district NEWTOWN | COUNTY OF NEWSHIRE

CHILD

1. Date and place of birth
Third March 1984
Newtown Hospital Newtown

2. Name and surname
John David SMITH

3. Sex
Male

FATHER

4. Name and surname
David Robert SMITH

5. Place of birth
Newtown, Newshire

6. Occupation
Accountant

MOTHER

7. Name and surname
Anne Jane SMITH

8. Place of birth
Newtown, Newshire

9. (a) Maiden surname
BROWN

(b) Surname at marriage if different from maiden surname

10. Usual address (if different from place of child's birth)
31 New Street, Newtown, Newshire

INFORMANT

11. Name and surname (if not the mother or father)

12. Qualification
Father

13. Usual address (if different from that in 10 above)

14. I certify that the particulars entered above are true to the best of my knowledge and belief

David Smith — Signature of informant

15. Date of registration
Eighth March 1984

16. Signature of registrar
Derek Jones

Figure 9: An example of a short birth certificate

District No.	Year *1984*	Entry No. *137*	NHS No.								

Birth registered in the district of

Newtown

1. Surname *Smith*	2. Sex
Names *John*	*Male*
David	

3. When born	4. Where born
Third March	*Newtown Hospital*
1984	*Newtown*

I hereby certify that the above particulars are extracted from a Register of Births in my custody.

Given under my hand this....*Eighth*....day of....*March*.......1984

.................................*Derek Jones*....................Registrar

District of....*Newtown*..

Figure 10: An example of an application form for a birth certificate

Applicant

Mr/Mrs/Miss	
Full postal address	
Telephone number	

Number of certificates required

☐ Full certificate ☐ Short certificate

Please tick appropriate box

☐ Birth register ☐ Adoption register

Surname at birth
Forenames
Date of birth
Place of birth
Father's surname
Father's forenames
Mother's maiden surname
Mother's forenames

You can also apply for a copy of a birth certificate by post, from the Office of Population Censuses and Surveys, General Register Office, PO Box 2, Southport, Merseyside, PR8 2JD. You will be sent an application form (*see* figure 10), which you fill in with the relevant details and return together with a cheque or postal order for £15.00. Applications by post take a little longer—you should allow 28 days for delivery.

Project

The next clue

Marriage certificates are also an essential source of information in your search. Every marriage certificate from 1912 onwards will contain the following information at the time of the marriage:

- the name of the male party
- the marital status of the male party (whether he was single, divorced or widowed)
- the address and occupation of the male party and the address and occupation of his father
- the name, address, marital status and occupation of the female party
- the name and occupation of her father
- the names of the witnesses to the marriage ceremony
- the place where the marriage took place

Before 1912 only the surname of the individual for whom the entry was made was recorded. If you are searching for marriage certificates before this date you will have to search index entries for both parties, but in this case you will need the surname of the male party and the maiden name of the female party. If the index number is the same for both names then you have the correct entry. It is also advisable to double-check if you are searching for the marriage certificate of somebody with a common name, especially if that marriage took place in a large town or city. For example, it is highly possible that more than one John Smith was married in London in a particular year.

Before 1870 the precise age of the parties in a marriage was not recorded—it was noted that the parties were 'of full age', but this can mean anything from 16 years onwards. After 1870 the age of both parties is given.

If, for example, you have searched for your grandparents' marriage certificate, you will be able to note down the maiden name of your grandmother (presuming that this was her first marriage) and details about her father. These pieces of information will help you search back even further. You will have a good chance of finding your grandmother's birth certificate and you will be able to find out where your great-grandfather lived and what his job was at the time of the marriage.

Project

Start a new tree

So you can see that you can now add some more clues to your file, which will enable you to start another tree of your mother's family. Your name will, of course, be on the bottom of this one too.

Project

Work further back

You can go on getting further back like this until 1837. As you get further back, it is as well to overlap the dates for births and marriages, as dates were not so reliably given in the old days, or the writing may not have been very clear, so inaccuracies might have crept in when they were copied. For example, if an eldest child is born in June 1839, include the years 1838, the probable year of the marriage, 1839 and 1840 in your search for a marriage certificate.

Remember, if you are trying to find the names of the parents of a child born in 1836, you will not find the record of this birth in St Catherine's House, but a child born later will have the information on his or her birth certificate.

Another detail you may come across in older certificates is the age given as 'minor' or 'full age'. Here you will have to guess ages, but 'minor' will mean under 21, and 'full age', anything over 21.

Project

Tracing the date

The procedure to trace a death certificate is the same.

Death certificates are indexed in the same way as births—so deaths before 1984 may not appear in the same quarterly index in which they occurred. Generally, death certificates are not of such value in a search as birth or marriage certificates. Before 1866 only the name of the deceased and the district in which the death was recorded appear. From 1866 to 1969 the date of birth of the deceased is also supplied, as given by the individual registering the death, although this may not always be accurate. From 1969 onwards, a more accurate date of birth for the deceased is given, where known.

So far our search has taken us along only our own path up the tree, and you may be wondering, for instance, how you could know whether there was an older child in the family, so you can work out the date of a marriage, or a younger one to give you information about parents who married before 1837. There are two main ways of doing this.

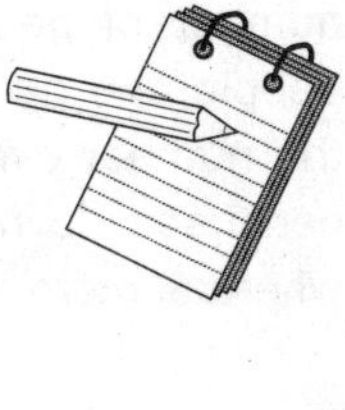

PART THREE

FILLING IN THE BLANKS

The Public Record Office in Chancery Lane is only a few minutes' walk from St Catherine's House, it was established in the 1850s to house the national records of England and Wales, which, before then, were scattered in various places. Government departments send their records, or censuses, here when they become about 100 years old, and they can be seen by the public free of charge.

The idea of a census is very old—you will probably have learned about the Domesday Book of 1086, which is the earliest recorded census in England. Since 1801 a census has been taken every 10 years (except in 1941). The oldest census records currently available for public inspection are from 1891. The last census carried out in the UK was in 1991—records of this census will not be made available to the public until the year 2091.

The census returns give us information on the number of people in the population, the ages of the people, the percentage of the population under 16 and the number over 65, etc, and their occupations. Earlier censuses do not contain so much reliable information, whereas more recent census returns give more details, such as the schools attended by the children in a household, and the number of rooms in a house.

Census returns may help you to fill in gaps in your search. Again it is important that before you start a census search you have made clear notes of all the information you have gained. Leaflets are available in the Public Records Office that will help you to narrow down your search, but the more information you have about your family and what it is you are searching for the easier and more successful your search is likely to be.

The census records are kept on microfilm, and you must obtain a reader's ticket to search them, but this is free. If you find census entries that provide relevant information then you can apply for a photocopy of them, which can be made for you for a small fee or which you can make yourself after buying a photocopy card.

If you are searching census returns for 1841 or earlier, it is important that you remember that the ages given for individuals were always rounded to the nearest 5 years. Therefore, if the age of John Smith is given as 40, it might be that his actual age at the time of the census was in fact 38.

Project

Bridging the gap

The first census records you will want to search are

those that will bridge the gap between the information you have already got from St Catherine's House and your next place of search, which will be the parish records (*see* Part Four). These are the census returns for 1841 to 1891.

It is possible to get information from the census returns from 1891 to the present day, but the search has to be made for you by an official, and you have to state in writing the name of the person for whom you are searching, the exact address, his or her relationship to you and the reason for the search. This search (or any other search undertaken on your behalf if you cannot make a personal visit) will cost £18.80. (*See* figure 11).

Year to be searched	Name	Address (number, street, village or town, district or city)
1891	*Joseph Smith*	*21 Green Street, Brighton*

Figure 11: An example of a search application form

Get permission first

You must also get the written permission of any of the individual's family who are still living, and state that any information you receive will not be used in any legal action. If the person named was not at the address you give on the night of the census, his or her name will not be on the form and you will not get any information.

In 1851 and 1861, even more details were given: the relationship of the people in the household to one another, their exact ages, whether married, fuller details of occupations, and, most important of all, the *exact* place of birth, like this:

1851 Census: 3, High Street, Ardenham, Sussex

Name	Relationship	Age	Occupation	Birthplace
William Smith	Head (m.)	71	Blacksmith	Ardenham
Mary Smith	Wife (m.)	67	Laundress	Shendon
David Smith	Son (m.)	40	Blacksmith	Ardenham
Elizabeth Smith	Dau.-in-Law	38	Dressmaker	Plumbley
William Smith	Grandson	14	Stoker	Ardenham
David Smith	Grandson	13	Apprentice tailor	Ardenham
Mary Smith	Grand-dau.	11	Seamstress	Ardenham
Elizabeth Smith	Grand-dau.	5		Ardenham

You will now see the importance of the census return to a genealogist, (which is the name given to those interested in tracing family trees).

Project

Clue to the parish

Work out gaps in your own family tree from the examples given above. For instance, from the census return you can see that the younger David was born in 1838, and his birth certificate will probably be at St Catherine's House. On this will be the names of the parents, but as he had a brother born in 1836, there is no trace of their marriage certificate. However, this census has given the parish of their birth and their ages, from which you can now work out their years of birth and make a search in the parish records where they were each born.

You also have the birth date and place of both his grandparents. This last piece of information will have taken you back to 1780, and you will probably be able to get even further back from parish records.

Project

Check each census

Check the returns from three censuses if possible, as there are sometimes members of the family who are in the earlier ones but had left home by the time a later census was taken. Ages were not always accurately given and can change from one census to the next. When searching a village, make a note of all the people of the same name in case there is a link. The same goes for cities and industrial towns, where many members of a family lived in the same road or district as each other.

Project

Keep a note

Make a note of all the *possible* clues as well as the definite ones, as these may be able to help you fill in any gaps in your tree with the aid of the parish records. You will now, have the names of all the other members of your family as well as your direct line, and you are now ready to start on the next stage of your investigation.

Project

Records to follow

Other records that may be of interest to you in the Public Record Office:

Pipe Rolls (1100-1837) these are accounts of payments made to the Crown, classified in counties.

Inquisitions Post Mortem (13th century–1645), a type of death duty on important tenants of the Crown.

Apprentice Records a stamp duty that was paid on

apprenticeship indentures. These records give the name of the apprentice, the name and trade of his master, the place of residence and the name of the apprentice's father, and his address.
Army Lists Muster Rolls, which began in 1708, are lists of men liable for military service (you must know the name of the regiment for these).

PART FOUR

LOOK INTO THE PARISH RECORDS

The next step in your search will take you to the parish where your ancestors lived. You will have found this out from St Catherine's House and the census returns. You may even have the names of two or three parishes to search, but they will probably be close to one another, because people did not tend to move far before about 1780, when families moved to the larger towns and cities to find work during the Industrial Revolution.

This search is the most exciting of all, because you will not only be in the original home of your ancestors, and perhaps able to see the actual houses where they lived and worked, but you will be able to handle old parish documents. If one of your family held a position of trust, such as that of a churchwarden, you may see records written in his own hand. These records are sometimes interspersed with personal comments and details of the weather.

Project

Get permission first

These records were kept in the parish chest, and you will need a magnifying glass for your search, as the records can be faded and difficult to read at times. The fee for a search of the parish chest is entirely up to the vicar, and as he or she may like to arrange for the verger or someone else to be present during your search, it is as well to write beforehand, asking for permission and enclosing a stamped addressed envelope for the reply.

The parish records referred to in this book are those of the Church of England which is the Established Church (the officially recognised Church) in England and Wales. Records of other denominations are kept separately (*see* Part Six).

It is difficult to trace families before 1500, unless they were royalty, landowners or land tenants, as no records were required before 1538. Even after 1538, records are sometimes difficult to trace as they were very erratically kept. In about 1597 they began to be kept on parchment instead of paper, and the clergy had to send copies to the bishops.

These copies are called Bishops' Transcripts, and are of great value to the searcher today as they are able, in some instances, to fill in gaps in parish registers.

Project

Go to the County offices

Many parishes have now transferred their old registers to the County Record Offices, where they are able to be seen free of charge and searched for as long as you like. You may also find that the Bishops Transcripts are also there, and as well as these records you will find a great many books and documents of local interest to help you.

Project

Learn old handwriting

You may find that very old records include some words or terms that you do not understand. Before 1620, Latin was widely used in parish records but you still might find later records that contain some Latin words. If you do come across these, or any other words that you are unsure of, write them down and then look them up in the language reference section of your local library.

It is also important to remember that, as these were church records of baptisms and burials, the dates that you find will not be the exact date of a birth or death—indeed it is possible that some people would not have been baptised for quite a few years after they were born.

There is a gap in the registers during the years of the Commonwealth of Oliver Cromwell, 1641–60. Many of the parish priests were relieved of their duties and the records put into the hands of laymen, many of whom were illiterate or disorganised. During this period people could get married before a justice of the peace and two witnesses, and not necessarily in a church, so marriage records are not complete. After the Restoration of the monarchy in 1660, the keeping of registers was handed back to the clergy.

Project

Look at the tombstones

The first place to search in the parish is the churchyard, so you will find that your magnifying glass comes in handy, and perhaps a soft brush, as old tombstones become weathered and covered in moss and need to be cleaned gently to be able to read the inscription. Take notes on all the inscriptions you can find relating to the family, and even take photographs of the clearer ones so that you can study them at your leisure. A great deal can be learned from them.

Project

Race for new clues

Very old family graves tend to be fairly close together, but if it is a large churchyard it is a good idea to ask your brothers and sisters and parents to help you. Each person could start from one corner of the churchyard and see who finds a clue first. In some parishes you may find that churchyards have been cleared of their gravestones. You may find them stacked around the walls, but, if not, you will probably find that a record has been kept of all the stones removed.

Project

Take your camera

Take photographs of all houses or plaques of interest to your family, and build up a dossier. It is fairly easy to trace the more prosperous members of a family and big landowners, but for information about humbler folk the parish records are an invaluable source of clues. Here you find records of rich and poor alike.

PART FIVE

A PEEP INTO THE PARISH CHEST

The parish chest, as the name implies, is the chest or box where all the parish records are kept. As the church played a very important part in the everyday life of the parishioners (something like the parish councils of today), it is full of great interest about people in the parish. Many records kept in the chest may date back before the beginning of the parish registers.

Project

Ask to see the banns

The dates of registers vary from parish to parish. Ask if you can also see such records as the churchwardens' accounts, settlement certificates, lists of inmates in local workhouses (which were recorded from 1722), pest houses (isolation hospitals for people with infectious diseases) and prisons. The register of banns, which gives the names of the parishes of both parties before marriage, are also kept.

Project

Ask to see the accounts

Churchwardens were responsible for the poor of the

parish, and all the details of their expenditure were recorded each year. Parish expenses for burying the very poor also went into the accounts. Illegitimate children were also a charge upon the parish, so often entries were recorded either entrusting them to the father, or making him marry the mother.

Project

Check the wanderers

Settlement certificates help to give information about the movements of parishioners from one parish to another. Every parish was responsible for the care of its poor and needy, so none wanted the extra burden of vagrants from other parishes. People moving from one parish to another had to provide a certificate giving their reasons for leaving and saying that they were settled in their previous parish and would be received back if necessary. These certificates date back to 1697.

Project

A clue in wool

In 1667, an act was passed that required all corpses to be buried in wool. This law was brought in to boost the woollen trade, but the custom gradually died out, and by the 18th century it was hardly ever done. While it was in force, however, an affidavit had to be signed to say the law had been complied with, and it was usually signed by a relative. Try to trace such an affidavit.

Other denominations—the burials of people of other religious denominations, with no burial grounds of their own, took place in the parish churchyard, but their records were kept separately (*see* Part Six).

In 17th-century registers just the name and village of the dead person tended to be given. In the next century ages were usually added and perhaps the occupation or relationship to another person, such as: 'Mary Smith, wife of David Smith, blacksmith of Ardenham'. From 1812, the place of residence was given: 'David Smith, 5, High Street, Ardenham, Blacksmith, aged 90'.

Many baptisms took place months or even years after births, so they do not help a great deal in your search, and you may find a double entry of baptism, one public and one private. The main interest in the entry of baptisms is the description of the father's occupation.

Project

Count the children

Try to trace the number in a family from the register of births. You may come across two entries of children with the same name, in which case you may find that the first child died before the birth of the second and so it was given the same name.

Unfortunately, as we have seen, marriage registers suffered a great deal during the Commonwealth. In 1754, however, a printed form was produced (*see* figure 12), on which marriages had to be recorded. You may find entries signed with an 'X', showing that either the bride or groom, or both, could not write.

______ of ______ Parish

and ______ of ______ Parish

were married this ______ by ______ with Consent of

______ this ______ Day of

______ in the Year One Thousand eight hundred and ______

By me ______

This marriage was solemnised between us { ______ / ______

In the Presence of ______

______

______

Figure 12

The printed form was the result of an act, called Lord Hardwicke's Marriage Act, which stated that marriages were not legal unless they were solemnised in church, either after banns had been called or by licence, and the church had to be that in the parish of either the bride or groom. This act applied only in England and Wales and exempted both Quakers and Jews.

Records of marriages are good from 1775, and the occupations of bride and groom are given from 1812. Before 1837, the names of the parents are rarely given, but where there are signatures of witnesses, they were usually relations, often brothers or sisters.

In the 17th century you will find entries like: 'David Smith and Mary Harris married', but in the late-18th century you get the details such as the names of witnesses, name of parish, occupation of both parties, and whether by banns or licence.

PART SIX

FAMILIES ON OTHER REGISTERS

If your family were not members of the Established Church of England, you will find their births, marriages and deaths, up to 1837, recorded separately, and the records were transferred to the Public Record Office in 1961.

A list of these registers before 1837 was printed and is called the 'List of the Non-Parochial Registers and Records in the Custody of the Registrar General' (1859). These are arranged by counties, and are in the Public Record Office. They include the records of the Huguenots who fled to this country, but not those of the Roman Catholics and Jews, who have kept theirs themselves.

Many Nonconformists (Protestants who do not belong to the Church of England) and members of other denominations met in secret, and some registers were kept of births and burials as well as other records, but there are few marriage registers before 1837 because, after 1754, no one could be married unless it was by a clergyman of the Church of England. This state of affairs lasted until 1837 but exempted both Quakers and Jews, who were allowed to marry according to the rites of their own church, and their registers are particularly well kept.

The records from 1837 are at St Catherine's House with all the other registers, a Royal Commission having been set up in that year. This was also the year that register offices were introduced to collect together all the registers of other denominations. Those not found in the list at the Public Record Office will have to be sought from the churches concerned.

Roman Catholics—Roman Catholics did not tend to keep records in the early days, and, having suffered considerable intolerance, are difficult to trace before 1832, which is when they were allowed their own places of worship.

Quakers—these records can be seen at the Library of the Society of Friends, Friends House, Euston Road, in London.

Jews—these records are kept at their individual synagogues, and they too were exempt from the law governing marriage by clergymen of the Church of England.

PART SEVEN

IF YOUR FAMILY COMES FROM . . .

You will have noticed that up until now this book has referred only to the records of England and Wales. This is because Scotland and Ireland hold their own registers of births, marriages and deaths, and also their public records. The search procedure is much the same as that in England and Wales, but the fees are different, and in the case of Scotland the records are very much more detailed although not quite so numerous.

Project

Where to start in Scotland

In Scotland the registration of births, marriages and deaths was not made compulsory until 1855. These registers, however, give much more information than those for England and Wales, and can be found at New Register House in Edinburgh. You are allowed to search the indexes for a small fee. Once you have found the relevant entry, you are then able to look at the register itself.

Male and female entries are kept separately, but all indexes are compiled yearly and include a note of the registration district. Many of the registration districts have changed over the years, but you can consult charts that will enable you to identify which district corresponds to which year.

Birth certificates for Scotland contain the following information:

- the child's name and address
- the date, place and time of the birth
- the names of the child's parents, including the maiden name of the mother
- the occupation of the father
- the date and place of marriage of the child's parents (though not for the years 1856–1860)
- the name and signature of the individual providing the information to the registrar

Death certificates for Scotland contain the following information:

- the name, age and address of the deceased
- the marital status of the deceased, including the name of a spouse on certificates from 1860 onwards
- the date, place and cause of death
- the names of the parents of the deceased, whether dead or alive, and the occupation of the father
- the name of the individual providing the information to the registrar and his or her relationship to the deceased.

The marriage certificates for Scotland also give more information (*see* figure 13).

District No.	Year 1982	Entry No.
Marriage in the district of Edinburgh		
1. When and where married	1982 July Twenty First Craighill (St Peter's) Parish Church, Edinburgh	
	Bridegroom	Bride
2. Surname	Brown	Clarke
Name(s)	Alan	Susan
3. Occupation	Retail Manager	Caterer
4. Marital Status	Single — 5. Date of Birth: Year 1957, Month 11, Day 23	4. Single — 5. Year 1958, Month 06, Day 03
6. Birthplace	Scotland	Scotland
7. Usual Residence	25 Gough Mews, Edinburgh	33 Craighill Lane, Edinburgh
8. Father's name(s) surname and occupation	Francis Brown Technician	Robin Clarke Baker
Mother's name(s) surname(s) and maiden surname	Elizabeth Brown m.s. McEwan	Sheila Clarke m.s. Green
9. Person solemnising the marriage	(Signed) Andrew Blair	(Designation) Minister
Witnesses and addresses	(Signed) Richard Sinclair 17 Glasgow Drive, Edinburgh	(Signed) Angela Moffat 23 Lincoln Street, Edinburgh
10. When registered	Year 1982, Month 07, Date 24	11. (Signed)........................ Registrar

Figure 13: An example of a Scottish marriage certificate

Census returns for Scotland are also kept in New Register House and can be searched for a fee.

WHERE TO START IN IRELAND

In Northern Ireland, the records for births and deaths from 1864 and marriages from 1922 are kept at the General Register Office, Chichester Street, Belfast. Records for marriages for the years 1864 to 1921 and non-Catholic marriages from 1845 are kept in District Registrar's Offices.

You can search the indexes for the registers for a fee, although your search time will be limited to a maximum of six hours and, if you are planning to make a personal visit, it is advisable to contact the General Register Office well in advance to arrange for your search. Otherwise you can arrange for a search for a specific entry to be carried out for you—you will have to pay a fee and provide sufficient information so that the staff can narrow down the search to a three-year period.

In the Republic of Ireland, the records for births, deaths and marriages are kept at the General Register Office in Dublin. These records cover births, deaths and marriages from 1864, and non-Catholic marriages from April 1845. Records up to 1922 cover all Ireland; after this date the records cover the Republic of Ireland only—those for Northern Ireland are kept in Belfast.

Census returns for Ireland are kept at the National Archives, Bishop Street, Dublin and the Public Record Office in Belfast. However, they may be of limited value. Those for the years 1901 to 1911 are open to the public but only fragments of earlier census returns remain, following a fire in the building where they were housed, in 1922.

Project

Other places to look

The Kirk Sessions Records in Scotland, which give notice of the arrival of persons into a parish from another parish and the reason, and also similar details of persons leaving the parish. These were kept by the parish ministers.

The Register of Sasines—this was a Scottish register showing the transfer of ownership of land, small cottages and crofts, was compiled from the 17th century. Often a ceremony would take place to mark this occasion, by the acceptance of earth and stone by the new owner. The registers are in three parts:

1 The Old Register of Sasines (1617–1868).

2 The Particular Register of Sasines—which covers the various counties.

3 The New General Register.

These are contained in many thousands of volumes

and are indexed for some counties. From 1781 there are abridged versions of the Sasines, which makes it fairly easy to trace ownership of the land from that date.

In Ireland compulsory registration came into force in 1864, even later than in Scotland. Unfortunately, they are not as detailed as the Scottish registers and, again, many of these records were also destroyed by fire.

PART EIGHT

WHERE THERE'S A WILL

After the parish records, wills are the most valuable source of information about families in earlier years. Apart from details of property, they may indicate the whereabouts of relatives who had moved away from the parish of their birth. They could also contain the names of unsuspected relatives. However, it is very important to remember that until quite recently wills were usually made only by those who were well off.

Sometimes confusion can arise in early parish records because of several men having the same name and living in the same town or village. Where his occupation or his wife's name is not mentioned, it is difficult to ascertain which is the man for whom you are looking. Wills can help to establish the right one.

It was unusual for a married woman to leave a will before the passing of the Married Women's Property Act in 1882, unless she was a widow. Before this act, a wife's possessions, except in certain circumstances, became her husband's on marriage.

Where a person died intestate, a term that means that he or she died without having made a will, letters of administration were taken out by the next of kin.

All these documents, which cover England and Wales, are also kept in the Principal Probate Registry in Somerset House.

Project

Your next search

Visit the Registry at Somerset House to carry out a search of wills made from 1858 onwards. The indexes are compiled alphabetically and by year, and these can be searched free of charge. Copies of the original documents can be consulted for a fee, and you can also obtain photocopies of these, again for a fee.

If you are unable to visit Somerset House, then you can make a postal application to the York Probate Subregistry, Duncombe Place, York, YO1 2EA. You will need to state the name and address of the dead person and the date on which he or she died. You will need to include a cheque or postal order for £2, made out to HM Paymaster General. No searches will be made on your behalf for wills over a century old.

Project

Look up an old will

Wills before 1858 are kept in another part of the Probate Registry, and searches must be made personally.

Some old wills make very interesting and amusing

reading. Early ones usually start with the words 'In the name of God, Amen', and then a short prayer for the soul of the writer. The amounts left in these old wills can be as little as 5p (one shilling in old money) a week for life. In some wills you may find bequests such as 'my best hat' or 'my second best shoes'.

Project

Go to your local library

Wills earlier than 1858 can be difficult to trace because of changes in parish boundaries, the proving of wills being in the hands of the church.

Ask your librarian if he or she knows of any books that might help you to locate a family will.

Project

More places to check

Briefly, proved wills fall into three categories. See if you can trace any wills in these:

1 If a man left property in one archdeaconry, which included several parishes, it went to the court of the Archdeacon to be 'proved'. These usually found their way into the care of the bishop of the diocese.

2 If property was left in two different archdeaconries, the will was 'proved' in the court of the bishop.

3 If property was left in two different dioceses, then it was 'proved' in the courts of either the Archbishops of Canterbury or York, depending on their area of jurisdiction.

Canterbury, the chief archbishopric, had the right to prove wills left in dioceses covered by both archbishoprics. Many of these wills go back to the 14th century, but records are not continuous until 1620, after which the records improve.

Indexes of Wills proved in the Prerogative Court of Canterbury (abbreviated to PCC) have been printed up to 1700, also the letters of administration. These records are now in the Public Record Office in Chancery Lane and include records of wills proved during the Commonwealth (1653–60).

Wills and administrations made in Wales prior to 1858 are held in the National Library of Wales in Aberystwyth. You will require a reader's ticket to use the search rooms.

Project

Wills in Scotland and Ireland

In Scotland many wills are kept at the Scottish Record Office in Edinburgh. Information is also available that will help you to locate wills that are held elsewhere. In Northern Ireland, the indexes of wills are kept at the

Public Record Office in Belfast. In the Republic of Ireland, indexes of wills are kept at the National Archives, Four Courts, Dublin, but again many of the relevant documents were destroyed by the fire in 1922. These records are not open to the public but you can arrange to consult the indexes in the reading room at the National Archives.

Project

Look at old newspapers

You may be able to get some information from old Irish newspapers, and there is a register of deeds that relate to the transference of land since 1708, some of which contain copies of complete wills or extracts, marriage settlements and mortgages. These are to be found in Henrietta Street, Dublin. *The Journal of the Irish Memorials Association* has thousands of inscriptions from tombstones, which may also help.

PART NINE

MORE CLUES TO FOLLOW

We have now looked at all the main sources for a search into your family background, but if you have had any difficulties, such as being too far away from the parish of your ancestors to be able to conduct a search, or if they were born abroad, there are still many other sources, particularly if you are able to get to London.

Project

Find out how a society can help

In England, the Society of Genealogists in London has, after many years of tireless work, built up extensive archives that can be searched by members of the public. These archives include copies of many parish records, which will be of particular value if you find that your ancestors lived in other parts of the country.

If you are searching for records in Scotland it might be worthwhile contacting the Scottish Genealogical Society in Edinburgh to see if they can help. If you are searching for records for Northern Ireland then the Irish Genealogical Project in Omagh, or the Irish Heritage Association might well be able to provide valuable help.

If you do not live near a genealogical society, then try a local history society—they may be able to provide you with information about your forebears and will certainly be able to provide you with interesting background material about where they lived.

Project

Compile a list

As you develop your search it is a very good idea to note down the places and people you have been to for help. You may find that your search lasts quite a long time and that you can only do a little every so often, particularly if you have to travel to find the information. So to make sure that you don't duplicate a search or waste time unnecessarily you could keep a personal diary. You could note down the date, what you were searching for, where you went to find the information, and, briefly, what you found. If you are visiting places where your ancestors lived, you could record your own impressions of that place.

Project

Try the British Library

You will need to satisfy British Library authorities that you are a genuine searcher before they will issue you with a reader's ticket. In this library you will find such books as the *Victoria County Histories*, tithe (church tax) redemption maps, early newspapers, records of people who were convicted for not attending Church of England services, and a complete set of *The Times* newspaper.

Newspapers might include the announcements of births, marriages and deaths which may not have been found in the parish registers. Those printed after 1801 are in the British Library in London.

Project

Find a library

The Guildhall Library in London contains many books of interest to the amateur genealogist, particularly those whose families lived in London. They are more accessible than those of the British Museum, and no reader's ticket is required. They have a good collection of London directories. Can you think of any library in your district giving similar facilities?

PART TEN

TRADES AND PROFESSIONS

If your ancestors belonged to particular trades or professions it is more likely that you will be able to find records and documents relating to them—so it is always worth noting down the occupation of an individual if you have found this in a census return or elsewhere.

Records of the clergy in the Church of England are among the easiest to find, since they were responsible for the keeping of records. These can be found in County Record Offices, or you could look up *Crockford's Clerical Directory*, which dates from 1858, or, if you are searching even further back, the *Index Ecclesiasticum*.

In Scotland, records of the Scottish Kirk Session are kept at New Register House in Edinburgh. It may be harder to trace the records of the members of other religious denominations.

The medical and legal professions are also easier to search. It is likely that the individual you are tracing will have academic and professional records. If you are searching for a member of the medical profession then try the registers of the university they attended and the records of the Royal College of Physicians and the Royal College of Surgeons and their Scottish equivalents.

Lawyers can be also be traced from university registers and, if they became a barrister (advocate in Scotland) or a judge, through court records.

Project

Trace some guilds

There were many guilds, such as the Butchers' Guild, the Tanners' Guild, the Shoemakers' Guild, to name but a few, and they all kept records of their members, which will be found in municipal records in your local record office. See how many guilds you can find in your area.

Most of the professions have their own records, so you can find many of these at the Public Record Office, or at their own record offices.

THE ARMED FORCES

If you are trying to trace an individual who served in the Army, the Royal Navy or the Marines, or the Royal Air Force, then there will almost certainly be a relevant record in existence.

If you are tracing army records it is very important that you know which regiment the individual served in, particularly if he was in the ranks. Regimental records of births, deaths and marriages are kept in the General Register Office at St Catherine's House. Other army records are maintained at the Public Record Office or the Army Record Offices. Records of officers can be found in the army lists at the Public Record Office at Kew. These date back to the beginning of the 19th century.

Naval records are rather more difficult to search. There is no shortage of records but it is hard to narrow down the search without the regimental system that exists in the army. However, it will help you if you know the name of the ship on which your ancestor served. Naval records (which date from 1749) are also maintained at the Public Record Office.

Records of men and women serving in the Royal Air-Force date from the early 1930s. Many are kept at the library of the Society of Genealogists, where non-members can search the indexes for a fee of £3 for the first hour and a smaller fee for each hour thereafter. Other records may be found at the Royal Air-Force Museum in Hendon, the Public Record Office or the Imperial War Museum. Again, the task will be much easier if you know which year you are searching for.

PART ELEVEN

START DRAWING

You should now be able to draw your family tree. You will need a large piece of paper, and you may even need to stick several together because your tree will not only have grown taller but spread as well, as some families tended to be very large. Once you have traced your family tree as far back as you can through the direct line from your father, you need not stop there.

Project

A new trail

You can set off on another trail and trace your mother's side of the family. This is known as the distaff side—the word 'distaff', being derived from the staff with which women once spun wool or flax. There is no end to the number of trees you can trace, but try only one at a time. Make notes on names you come across on a tombstone or in a parish register, as it may save you a journey when you start on your next quest.

Project

The times they lived in

Once each tree is complete, you could get coloured pens

and draw the direct line you are tracing in red, and put the rest in blue or black. Leave a wide margin on either side, and put the names of the reigning monarch of each generation on one side, and on the other a list of all the great events that took place during that monarch's reign.

You could also make sketches of the type of dress worn in each different generation—try to find an illustrated book on costumes and fashion through the ages in your local library.

Project

Meaning of your name

Many of our modern surnames are directly related to some of the characteristics of our ancestors, perhaps by reference to their trade, like Smith, Carpenter, Mason or Baker, their physical features, like Short, Little or White, and even their address, like Townsend, Meadows or Field.

Over the years some of these original names have become slightly altered. Smythe will once have been the more humble Smith, and Blake perhaps Black. The building of the hereditary surname was a gradual process. The first description could have been 'son of', which later became tacked on to the father's name, like Richardson. The prefix 'Fitz', also means 'son', being a derivation of *fils*, the French for 'son'.

In Scotland, clansmen took the name of the clan, and the prefix Mac means son'. In Wales, the word for son is 'ap', so we get ap Howell turning to Powell. See if you can work out the origin of your own surname.

Note: From Spring 1997 the records currently housed at the General Register Office at St Catherine's House and the Public Record Office building in Chancery Lane will be transferred to Myddelton Place, Myddelton Street, Islington, London EC1R 1UW. For further enquiries contact the Office for National Statistics on 0171-396-2828.

LET'S INVESTIGATE!

Titles in this series:

1 Making Musical Instruments
2 Conjuring
3 Fossil Hunting
4 Being an Inventor
5 First Aid
6 Mapping the Night Sky
7 Ponds and Aquariums
8 Your Dog
9 Your Cat
10 Small Pets
11 Collecting
12 Painting in Watercolours
13 Tracing your Family Tree
14 The Weather
15 Drawing